My Sweet Valentine

Edited by

Heather Killingray

First published in Great Britain in 1997 by
ANCHOR BOOKS
1-2 Wainman Road, Woodston,
Peterborough, PE2 7BU
Telephone (01733) 230761

HB ISBN 1 85930 505 9
SB ISBN 1 85930 500 8

FOREWORD

Anchor Books is a small press, established in 1992, with the aim of promoting readable poetry to as wide an audience as possible.

We hope to establish an outlet for writers of poetry who may have struggled to see their work in print.

The poems presented here have been selected from many entries. Editing proved to be a difficult task and as the Editor, the final selection was mine.

St Valentine's Day is reputedly the day on which birds find their mates; yet it is more renowned as the day of the year when anonymous admirers send tokens of their affections to those whom they cherish.

Poetry is an intimate and personal mode of communication - it allows the discreet and romantic expression of thoughts and emotions. Plato claimed 'Every man is a poet when he is in love' - a very apt phrase, emphasising the fact that poetry is created from strong emotions . . . love . . . A poem is hence the ultimate Valentine's gesture.

I trust this selection will delight and please the authors and all those who enjoy reading poetry.

Heather Killingray
Editor

CONTENTS

Love And Time	Philip Smith	1
Untitled	Rachel Henderson	2
Love Changes Everything	Terri Annable	3
Do They Know	J Bishop	4
My True Love	Carol Rees	5
Love	Penny Osborne	6
Love At First Sight	Duncan Uist Fisher	7
My Love	M J Tuffin	8
My Love	June Woodward Martin	9
Ramblings Of A White Witch	Angela Anderson	10
Love Song	Jack Withers	11
Untitled	Sylvia Currey	12
As Long As My Heart Keeps On Beating	M Prickett	13
Love's Bloom	Joanne G Wilding	14
Love	Marie Chapman	15
Love	Susanne McNamara	16
Memories	Maria McLuckie	17
My Love For You	M Newnes	18
The Day	David Beastall	19
The Clock	Tania Cheslaw	20
Valentine For My Husband	Mary Warnock	21
Love Is Forever	P Robinson	22
Summer Love	Eve Logan	23
Ahead Of Time	Brenda Elvery	24
Without You	Gwen Norman	25
Endlessly Mine	G Thompson	26
Loves Attention	Claire Richardson	27
Love	Joan Cason	28
First Love	Tanya Stephen	29
Parting Kiss	Steve Albert	30
Love Poem	Simon Cartlidge	31
Memories	Marian Kerr	32
Our Treasure	Julie Sanderson	33
The Power Of Love	Rhonda Ferguson	34
Love Is A Peach	Elizabeth Hopkins	35

Our Anniversary's	Marjorie Johnson	36
Sincere Feelings	Kevin P Collins	37
Beryl By Candlelight	David Robertson	38
Love	Joyce Croot	39
Love Can Change All Life	F Higgins	40
No Time To Love	Amanda M Lunsden	41
Oscillations	Yvonne Chamberlain	42
Love Messages	Lucy Davies	43
Undiscovered Love	Sher Alam	44
A Merseyside Love Poem Kathryn Shirley	Brian Reck	45
Spread Your Love	Margaret Blackwell	46
On Valentine's Day	Lucy Carrington	47
Destiny	Clare Johnson	48
Love Search	Mary Tappenden	49
A Letter To Helena	Jennifer Polledri	50
Thank You For Loving Me	Helen Georgeou	51
Love	Rebecca Eira Davies	52
Though Spiders Ride The Wind	Sandra Lewis	53
A Red Rose	Marjorie Spokes	54
A Dream Of Love	Cecil Cundell	55
Friends Not Lovers . . .	Gill Price	56
Pisces	Judith Spencer	57
Love	Jaki Holden	58
Untitled	D Devlin	59
Love	Margaret Busst	60
Love's Garden	J M Butler	61
Like The Back Of Your Hand	Colin Black	62
Loving You	David Pickett	63
One Look At You	Pauline Launt	64
Endless Love	R Warrior	65
My Husband	Carole Dicker	66
Time Was	J Hawkes	67
Goodbye	Patricia Chilver	68
New Love	Enid Phillips	69
Creator Of My Eden	Hannah Bird	70
Love	Matthew Pearson	71
All I Ever Want	Maria Diana	72

Dream Desire	S Smith	73
The Lovers	Charlene Taylor	74
Love	Stella Duff	75
You	M Grigg	76
Valentine Message	Gwyneth Murphy	78
Leaving	Richard Croke	79
I Can't Decide	Kate Turner	80
Quiet Love	Charles McGinness	81
My Partner	Terry Baldwin	82
Love Makes No Sense	S Jackson	83
My Valentine	Eve de Groot	84
Dear Love	Pamela Gooding	85
The One I Love	Victoria Elliott	86
Misty Morning Valerie	K Newport	87
My Love	A Clark	88
The Chains Of Love	Bernice Evans	89
Four Words	Keith Morgan	90
My Love	Barbara Hussey	91
An Opening	Christine Rogers	92
Starlings	Ben Verinder	93
Love Is . . .	Rebekah Hudson	94
Our Love Is True	Ricky McNeill	95
Dark Horse	Dragon	96
Untitled	Elaine Briscoe-Taylor	97
Regrets	J Hopkins	98
Forever There	Glenn B Liddle	99
Precious Time	Josephine Aldred	100
Felicity	Bryn Bartlett	101
Card To Angel's Camp - USA	Allyson Kennedy-Kiddle	102
You	Tammara M Wilband	103
I Truly Do	Richard Reeve	104
There Was A Soul	Gabley Copperston	105
I Miss You	Stephen Maughan	106
I Look At You As Through A Window . . .	Jack Crossman	107
Love Of My Life	Gibson Forbes	108
Love's Old Story	Philip J Ellis	109
Where Did Love Go?	Edgar Wall	110

Love . . .	Glen Johnson	111
Au Revoir	Ashley P Loasby	112
A Description Of My True Love	Shirley Ann Downing	113
Duty Kisses	I M Williams	114
The Old Sailor	A T Lammiman	115
I Remember You	Darren Moody	116
Wrong	Marda	117
Love	Melissa Perez	118
What Is Love	Danielle Turner	119
Lovers	Ann Dulon	120
381	Roseanna May	121
Lack Of Love	L Marshall	122
He Does Not Know	L Higgins	123
Questions	William L I Newman	124
Love Has Flown	Bruce Ward	125
Journey	Peter Cranswick	126
Words Unspoken	Mary Brooke	127
More Fish In The Sea	Delia Marheineke	128
From The Darkness	Karen Mather	129
Until	Martin Goldsmith Silk	130
The Grand Romancer	Emily Johnson-Rodgers	131
The Span	Pat Jones	132

LOVE AND TIME *1ST PRIZE WINNER*

There is a time in everyone's life
When we are romantically overwhelmed with emotion
The caring, the feeling, the love we want to share
With that one individual who generates such warmth inside
It is a time of communications and expression
Phone calls and writing, letters and poetry
Thinking about each other, sharing time together
Holding hands, kissing, touching, the warmth of love

For some it is short and on reflection shallow
Tainted with blindness of reality, in hindsight gullible
But the many experience the joy of sustained togetherness
The years roll by and the flame still burns bright
The outward expression, the holding hands, the kissing
Falls into decline as does the true communication of feeling
Replaced by records of events, playback of the day
And yet the feeling, the comfort the trust is still there
On occasions it is shown and shared
As we take stock of the love, so much taken for granted

Love can wear and fade like a pair of slippers
So often we don't realise 'living' needs to be worked at
Interaction, sharing, loving and growing together is natural
But should never be taken for granted or assumed
The feeling, for life and in life is precious
And so when time ticks by and the pace of life quickens
We still need to find time, thought and words for our loved ones.

Philip Smith

Untitled

You were there
Just sitting, talking
You looked up
You saw me
You smiled

My heart melted.

Rachel Henderson

Love Changes Everything

We sing 'Love changes everything',
It's just a gently gnawing pain.
Cupid's darts that pierce my heart
Bring sunshine out of rain.
But soon the storm-clouds gather,
Love trickles slowly away.
I'm left to weep while shadows creep
And darkness shrouds my day.

Terri Annable

Do They Know

Do they know I miss love
And sharing with you.
Do they know I keep secrets
Of things I would do,
If you were with me.

Your smile that I've lost
The touch of your hand.
Returns to me daily
As tide washes sand,
Yesterday's thoughts are here.

Do they know I miss love
And laughing with you.
Do they know I keep secrets
Of memories true.
Returning to me.

My life now is seen
As aged and spent
My years spiral backwards
Today's, only lent
Till our reunion again.

Do they know I miss love
And being with you
Do they know I keep secrets
Of things I will do .
When you come for me.

J Bishop

My True Love

(To Alan)

You gave me a rose,
I gave you my heart.
You gave me your life,
I vowed we would never part.
I remember when we met at a local dance
For us it was a true romance.
We danced to the music of knock on wood,
I know the exact spot where we stood.
My dreams all came true when we fell in love,
That special night as the stars glowed above.
You gave me carnations of red and white,
For you my darling it was love at first sight.
You gave me a ring you won at the fair,
It proved to me how much you did care.
Caresses and kisses showered upon me,
Our love was meant to be.
I love you now as I loved you then,
You had to have me home before ten.
We had a great wedding day,
I loved you more than words can say.
You gave me five gifts of love and joy,
Three beautiful girls and two wonderful boys.
I love you more than life itself
Much more than any kind of wealth.
Sharing our thoughts, and memories too,
My darling I love you, I truly do.

Carol Rees

LOVE

The air is heavy almost like my
heart, waiting for something that
will never be, to want is not
to have to love is to want.
Too much.

Penny Osborne

Love At First Sight

In a hustling, bustling bar, she sits in the distance
A mutual glance in an incredible instance
Love at first sight?
Or merely the mood of the night?

My feelings are strong - I think hers are too
We're not oil and water, but like paper and glue
Her face and body, a work of art
With all the requirements of a potential sweetheart

Come over. Let's embark in conversation
Put my mind at rest and confirm my infatuation
To get chatting so soon. It'd be stupid
Or have we become the latest victims of cupid?

Like a magnet and metal she comes my way
With a mission in mind - something to say
An aura, a question over which I ponder
Her sweet sounding words making me fonder and fonder

Two years on from that nostalgic night
Exists a righteous relationship with not one fight
Or disagreement but an array of affection
A relationship formed by more than a predilection.

Duncan Uist Fisher (16)

My Love

My love for you is Oh so true
I idolise everything you do
You capture everybody's heart,
I've loved you from the very start.

You've got eyes of blue, skin so fair,
features so fine and very dark hair.
I can't believe how lucky I am,
I'll always be your number one fan.

My hair is blonde, my eyes are brown
I never want to put you down.
The age gap between us is just two years
the closeness we share dispels all fears.

I hope we'll always feel this way,
As you grow older, you'll have your say.
I hope you'll feel the way I do
and love me as strongly as I love you.

I'll take care of you as we mature,
of my love, there is no cure.
You're my baby sister - there is no other,
I'll stay true to you, because I'm your brother.

M J Tuffin

My Love

I am reminded of another night some time ago
When I wrote to you because I loved you so
My place was then at another man's side
So my feelings for you I had to hide
The ache deep inside is just the same
Cupid certainly knew just where to aim
I long for your touch, to hear the sound of your voice
If the phone would just ring I would rejoice
No sleep last night without your tender care
Some sleep and comfort tonight is my only prayer.

June Woodward Martin

RAMBLINGS OF A WHITE WITCH

You touched me first my sweetest love,
I think it was a dream,
You came at last to free me, a belated celestial scheme.
You lay silently behind me, my hands by yours possessed
I'd yearned for you my darling, you came at my behest.
I saw you in the moonlight, tender grass was moist with dew,
I raised my arms above me and entrusted me to you.
From moonlight into darkness, I knew you would be there.
I'd belonged to you so long ago, before you seemed to care.
Your cherished face before me, your hand reached out for mine,
Joyous in the knowledge that our hearts and souls entwined.
Enchanted then and now, it feels like coming home,
Drowning in this love for you, without you is alone
Sinking, kissing you my love, should something come to sever
You touched my soul, you have my heart, this love goes on forever.

Angela Anderson

Love Song

You were my venue, you were my cue,
You were the one who knew what was true.
You were too often another me, yet another closed avenue.

You loved me and I loved you
But neither of us could adjust to the human zoo.

You were someone,
You were that other one
You were the one who loved to have fun.

You were commanding, you were demanding,
You rent asunder any understanding.

You were my shadow and my echo,
You were deep whilst I was shallow.

Terrifyingly intense you gave life sense,
I was banal when you were immense.

You were busy where I was lazy,
But I blame you for making me go crazy.
Earth-mother and smothering lover.
Such is nature.

Jack Withers

UNTITLED

When two people can live as one,
They share the sorrow and the fun.
When you can read each others mind
And just the right words you can find.
When one is sick you feel their pain,
You share both a loss and a gain.
When one does well, you fill with pride
And from them your worries you can't hide.
You can share memories from long ago,
Learn to say yes, when you really mean no.
Sharing the shores of a foreign land
Walking, strolling, hand in hand.
And when the hair starts turning grey,
You know what the other is going to say.
When love's young dream lingers on,
When hearing the words of that special song.
A knowing look, or just a glance,
Whilst doing the steps of your favourite dance.
Of each other being sure, without a doubt
That is what love is all about.

Sylvia Currey

As Long As My Heart Keeps On Beating

I didn't believe in love at first sight
Until I saw your face.
I wanted to get to know you
before you vanished without a trace.
But I was too shy to speak to you
the thought just made me blush,
So I kept my emotions all in track
as you walked away in a rush.
I have seen you often since
that very first time.
But still the silence I keep
and every time you walk away
my eyes just want to weep.
But there is one thing that's certain
there is one thing that's true
As long as my heart keeps on beating
I know I will always love you.

M Prickett

Love's Bloom

Our love is like a flower
That has grown from a seed
First friendship like the leaves
That allow the plant to breathe!

The first kiss, that like a rose bud
Gives a hint of the wonder to come
That opens and shows its full glory
Basked in the warmth of the sun!

But where roses sadly fade
And eventually die away
Our love will continue to blossom
Way beyond our dying day!

Joanne G Wilding

LOVE

Love, can be, a certain thing -
Often, hits you, in the spring,
For, it's when, we're unaware,
Cupid's arrows, fly the air!

Unsuspecting victims, find, -
Passion changes, many a mind,
What, he dips, his arrow in,
Eros, is almost, sure to win!

Alas, as winter, comes around -
Hearts, can plummet, to the ground,
Love, not guaranteed to last,
Will die, in spite-of, darts well cast!

Marie Chapman

LOVE

Love is like an ocean.
Love is like a heart.
Love is covered in lotion
and she is my sweet-heart.

Love is like a cloud
high in the sky
Love is like a sound
Where my love is found.

Love!

Susanne McNamara

MEMORIES

Eyes filled deep, with love and truth
Promises fulfilled since way back in youth
Held together in low and high winds.
Held tighter, in the hurricanes
Dripping with love, well worth the fight
After pulling through those rains and feeling sunlight.
Music filled our hearts as we walked along the shore.
Memories buried deep in its core
Treasured, as they will always be
Memories, memories never set free.

Maria McLuckie

My Love For You

My love for you is the feeling I get deep down in my heart.
My love for you is the feelings of sadness when we are apart.
My love for you is the feelings as my heart just skips a beat,
Everytime you enter the room and each time that our eyes meet.
My love for you is feelings I will never understand,
I only know that it's grown since you gave me my wedding band.
And as the years will come and go, I'll keep your love in store
Along with mine, deep in my heart
And love you forever more.

M Newnes

THE DAY

The day has finally arrived
I sit contemplating the moment
Outside the air is dank and cold
But a warm glow pervades my being
Shapes and reflections, pass me by
As I move nearer to you in distance and time.

My awareness is heightened
And my imagination takes over
How will you look, what will you say,
The moment of truth arrives and I
Am feeble of word to describe it
'Radiant' 'Beautiful' - words
Which hardly do you justice.
Reality slowly gains control over
My conscious thoughts,
Space and time have yet to converge,
But I know, for I have seen, and been
With my goddess of love.

David Beastall

THE CLOCK

I waited for you by the clock
Just as we agreed
But with every tick and tock
I wondered if you'd heed
My every wish and every prayer
The call I placed to get you there

And as the minutes came and went
My heart beat faster
And I sent
A million tiny kisses by
Which to hurry you to my side

As the clock struck onto eight
I knew that you would not be late
And then I saw you driving by
As ever eager to supply
Me with hugs and kisses hot

But what is this
Have I been shot
With arrows sent from heaven above?
You've brought the chocs . . . Oh my love!

Tania Cheslaw

Valentine For My Husband

A valentine poem for my darling
A special day for him
To celebrate the times together
We've had though thick and thin

Now we are growing older
Our love will never die
Because our love was destined
From God above 'He knows why,'

Our years together have been happy
And a lot of the world we've seen
But our favourite place is Italia
For the wonderful sights we have seen

But back again to my darling
That wonderful wonderful man
He's good, he's kind, he's faithful,
And will help whoever he can

So today on this valentine day
I wish him a lovely time
Because a man like him is hard to find
And he's mine, mine, mine.

Mary Warnock

LOVE IS FOREVER

All my love, I give to you sweetheart
I give it with all my heart,
And it will last through all the years
Until death, do us part.

I've loved you for so long now
You're everything to me,
At my side in all I do
To have to hold and to see.

Your loving kiss is tender
Like a petal on a rose
You're always warm and loving
That's real love I suppose.

The years have gone swiftly by
My love for you still grows.
I love you now, I always have
Till the end of time, 'who knows'.

P Robinson

SUMMER LOVE

In hazy days replete with love,
We lie together in cool, dark grasses,
And the whisperings of butterfly wings surpasses
The cuckoo's call above.

In the warm haven of your bosom,
I watch the dandelion seed float in the breeze
Towards the glade, into the shade of trees
Festooned with summer blossom.

And lying here in summer field,
In the secrets of your arms for hours,
Droning bees collect with ease from flowers
The nectar that they yield.

Inside the recesses of your heart
I find your love entwined with summer madness.
But chilly evening invades, persuades with sadness
That now we must part.

Eve Logan

AHEAD OF TIME

Our footprints left upon the sand
As we walked on hand in hand
Would we stay together for life?
Or maybe he'd find another wife,
We skipped along, happily now
So much in love, it showed and how
With cheeks aglow and eyes so bright
Not caring if it was day or night.
Stopping to kiss, hearts beating fast
Wishing this moment to ever last
Planning ahead and dreaming as one
Years to follow with so much fun
Running on now arms entwined
A lot can happen in that time.
Because as you really ought to see
He was only four and I was three.

Brenda Elvery

Without You

Without you all the birds would cease their singing.
Without you every stream no song would trill.
No bells with silvery chime would swing a-ringing,
And no more spring with joy my heart would fill.

No country scene with blue smoke softly winding
Away up in the greenness of the trees.
Nor white sails gleaming brightly, swiftly winging
Their way through wavelets ruffled by a breeze
Would stop my heart to realise their beauty.
Without you I would miss such dreams as these.

Yet let me walk beside you, feel your nearness,
And I should notice wonderingly again,
Each beauty as it came in wind or sunshine
Or dripping softly from a shower of rain.

Let me just place my hand in yours for always,
And know that not again will we two part.
To hear you say 'I love you' and to mean it
To know that you have given me your heart.
These are the joys I ask, just to be happy,
Together and a new life ours to start.

Gwen Norman

ENDLESSLY MINE

I waited so long it seemed for you,
I thought my dream would never come true.
I saw you for the first time and away went my fears,
But secretly my heart was weeping tears.

I was all mixed up and didn't know what to do,
Cradling you in my arms, I could only hold on to you.
Life could hold no greater treasure,
As you, my darling, have brought so much pleasure.

All too soon you have grown,
However, the seed of my devotion has been sown.
I know I must share you with one or another,
But no-one can replace you in the heart of your Mother.

As you tread life's highway, as I know you must,
In God and me place your trust.
Some days I will rant and rave,
Don't reject me though, your cuddle I will crave.

I adore all your maddening little ways,
And whilst we grow older together there will be good and bad days.
But one thing is everlasting and will not falter,
My love for you is strong and will never alter.

I gaze down at you often in silent adoration,
You are God's masterpiece, His creation,
He has seen fit to send you to me,
And I will love you endlessly, endlessly, endlessly . . .

G Thompson

LOVES ATTENTION

Practising my smile in the mirror
For the boy who won't look my way
Preening my hair 'though it's perfect
And memorising what I'm going to say

I know that I'll never speak to him
It's all just a game to me
'Cause I'm too shy to ever go near him
If only he'd look over to see

That I'm not just a girl who keeps smiling
It's because I'm so shy you see
We could be a wonderful couple
Please, just for once *notice me!*

Claire Richardson

LOVE

What is love does anyone know
It is a feeling that will come and go
Love, love what can it be
It is something we cannot see.

A feeling that happens to young and old
Many a tale of love can be told
It's happened since the world began
Between a woman and a man.

We say it with flowers and a ring
With anticipation what it might bring.
The family can bring us love and joy
The birth of a girl or a boy.

The love of life and beautiful things
The love of money and the pleasure it brings
We give love to animals and friends
True love we give just never ends.

Love we all should find someday
And make all hate just fade away.
A perfect world in which to live
With all the love we each can give.

Joan Cason

First Love

Wrapped in abundance of love and cuddles
Makes me feel kinda special
Kinda nice

My stomach is like a whirlpool
When I see you approaching near

My head is like a feather when you gently
Kiss my ear

My heart beats faster - faster like a tribal drum

My teeth go all gooey like pieces of
Sticky gum

My body trembles, sending shivers
down my spine

This is what happens when I look at
You each and every time.

Tanya Stephen

PARTING KISS

Their parting kiss was on a lonely mountain
but their love still flowed
an eternal fountain
from ice to desert
their story's told
not knowing their fate
or how it would unfold

he kissed her vision
she held to his memory
their paths divided
but their souls winged the skies
for their love it never dies

on misty mornings their shadows tread these glades
their parting kiss lingers still
their last touch at the dawn of time
hand in hand a tryst divine

on deserted moors and barren hills
where the crows lament
and dead elms despise the sun
hope yet lays buried awaiting their return

for on a far-off silvered shore
they meet again
a fleeting assignation
lovers' footprints
twined tracks in the sand

they beckoned not fate
their love must wait
as they walk through the surf
parting once more
till the new dawn kisses again
this long lost shore.

Steve Albert

LOVE POEM

Be gentle with your sudden moods
Be soft like pillows, a faith that soothes
Allow me some more time to speak
Of your golden hair of these tears I weep.

Make not home for idle chat,
For arguments, for this and that
Spare some time to ease my pain
Show me your heart and I'll love again.

Simon Cartlidge

MEMORIES

Bunches of snowdrops
White as snow
To a resting place will go,
With memories of loved ones
I love you so.

Marian Kerr

Our Treasure

The clock strikes midnight
Outside there's no light
But I'm in your arms
You're hugging me tight

Your arms offer comfort
Your voice calms me too
When there's thunder and lightning
I'm glad I'm with you

As I snuggle closer
I hear your heart beat
As rain patters down
Outside on the street

Soft hands stroke my hair
Relaxing me so
You make me feel sleepy
How only you know

Your lips kiss my forehead
My heart skips a beat
Strong arms hug me gently
As I fall to sleep

Julie Sanderson

The Power Of Love

In a world of hate and greed and evil
That with them drag you down,
And all the cold and lonely cities
Where people like machines hurry round,
And all the nights of silent screaming
With the pain inside your mind
You wonder how love can survive
In this all-consuming mire.

In a world hell-bent on self-destruction,
And a government that doesn't care,
Cold evil stalks its bitter prey,
And at it, it doth tear
But like a snowdrop in the springtime
Pushing through the frozen ground,
Your loving brought me to you
Like a lost soul who's been found.

Like the light within the darkness
You set fire to my soul
And our love will chase away the shadows
Which once upon us stole.
In your arms the world is perfect,
Without you is only pain.
You who taught me to believe in love
Are my reason for staying sane.

Rhonda Ferguson

Love Is A Peach

I have watched my love all summer through,
Like a peach ripening on the bough;
At first, a trifle acid,
Then mellowing and blooming into full maturity.
Oh! How I long to sink my lips -
My very soul,
Into depths, sweet and heavenly.

Elizabeth Hopkins

Our Anniversary's

I'm glad our anniversary's here,
It gives me chance to say
How very much you mean to me,
In a special kind of way.

And if I could paint a rainbow
Or a sky of vivid blue,
Or fetch some pearls up from the sea,
I'd do all these things for you.

Because you have made me happy
In a precious year that's flown
But I am even happier now
Because our love has grown.

There is an understanding now
That we both have come to know,
And you are my life, my love, my all,
And my heart just loves you so.

Marjorie Johnson

SINCERE FEELINGS

The feelings in my heart, I have for you.
Comes with gentleness, and love so true.
Sincere feelings, a world of the truest love.
Given to me, for you, by the angels above.

Love given to you, by this lowly man.
Would give you the world, if he can.
Your eyes so blue, the colour of the sky.
In a world of pain, some lonely hearts cry.

The truest of sweet love, I get from you today.
In my heart forever, you will always stay.
Hope and laughter, you have given to me.
You are my only one, and forever will be.

Love, happiness and laughter, you fill up my life.
I am forever grateful, that you became my wife.
A love like yours, will be mine forever more.
As waves of happiness, will kiss a lonely shore.

No man could be happier, as I am today.
Two hearts overflowing with love, will always stay.
Our love is endless, fills the tide of time.
You and I together, you'll always be mine.

Kevin P Collins

Beryl By Candlelight

The mirror on the wall, shows a deflection, gives a reflection.
And I see - Beryl by candlelight.
She looks alright, to me tonight.
Beryl by candlelight, 'neath the flame so bright, she's mine tonight.
But, if that flame should die, I know then, I should cry.
So, candle, please burn so bright.
An help me fight, for her love tonight.
Candle, please burn so bright, and stay slight, for me tonight.
But, as the flame burns down, and as I look around, just like the flame
- She's gone.

David Robertson

LOVE

Love is like a gentle tune
that never goes away
Gentle as a summer breeze
as sweet as new mown hay
Love can never fade away
'tis like a stabbing pain
through your heart it goes
to make your heart a-flutter
and when you've seen that
seemly chap your legs they
turn to butter
Love is like a butterfly
going from flower to flower
Ah! I wish I had a chap
to love and treasure this hour.

Joyce Croot

Love Can Change All Life

As I sit here by my fireside
My thoughts are all with you
I look outside my window
And the sun comes shining through

My eyes saw naught but misery
My ears heard sorrow and fear
My heart felt only sorrow and pain
My soul lost in the bleakest night

Where once were clouds is now pure light
Where once was rain is now dry land
Where once despair is now all bright
Where once was pain an open hand

How can it be that things all change
And is it true that love shines through
Oh yes my friend these things can be true
As long as you let your heart fly free

And since we met my heart flies high
Wherever it will over all the land
Without restrictions nor jealous tie
It needs only love to guide its way

My love for you has brought these things
Which make my life so glad and pure
As my soul speaks to you without any fear
To tell you of a love to last through all the years.

F Higgins

No Time To Love

Sitting and waiting,
Been waiting four years.
Sharing the memories
Sharing the fears.
I'm starting to feel
All is not right.
Why am I sitting
Alone every night?
Time to reflect
Is all very well
Am I in heaven?
Or a journey through hell?
To gain more attention
I often have tried.
But your work won't permit it
Leaves loving aside.
We both are attached
One to the other
But no so much lovers
As sisters and brothers.
I tried and I tried
To be understanding
But all I can be
Is a lot less demanding.
You say that you want me
and all that is mine.
I just can't understand
How you don't have the time!

Amanda M Lunsden

OSCILLATIONS

With tears in my eyes
I can't tell you lies
These words must be spoken
With a lump in my throat
I can but hope
No-one's heart will be broken.

You play me at will
And take of your fill
Then leave me depleted
I do need you so
Yet still I don't know
How you need it completed.

With a touch of your hand
You give me command
I do nothing but follow
An inflection of voice
And I have no choice
Still to believe in tomorrow.

And then you take back
What I sadly lack
The assurance you gave yesterday
My thoughts and emotions
Give me strange notions
Of escape and running away.

But that I love you
The one only thing true
Can never be taken away
So please just forgive me
Let me be free
Join me in loving today.

Yvonne Chamberlain

Love Messages

The day was right, the time had come,
For you to unite and become one.
You've been through the rough,
But mainly the smooth,
Times have been happy,
As you have both proved.
I send you my love,
From the bottom of my heart.
To wish you both happiness,
That will forever last.

Lucy Davies

UNDISCOVERED LOVE

I am lost in my love for you
Which way could I safely turn
Should I prolong this love
Or let this undiscovered love burn.

I want to liberate this love
Confined inside my heart
Perhaps I could share it with you
Perhaps you could love me too.

If only you could say just once
You have fallen in love with me
I would become the happiest person in the world
Happiness for all mankind to see.

But whether you love me or don't
Change my love for you, it won't
The position you rest inside my heart
This nobody is able to see
My love for you will endure for eternity.

. ***Sher Alam***

A Merseyside Love Poem
Kathryn Shirley

Semi-detached houses and green privet hedges,
Trees on the pavement in nice even rows.
Small neat gardens and tools on the ledges
Of the garage, where her dad comes and goes.

How it was we started to go out,
I can't recall in exact detail now,
There seemed to be a host of friends about,
Before I had the pluck to call her 'Scho'.

We first met at the height of summertime,
The recollection of her cool brown face,
Is like a Durer picture, engraved on my mind,
That even the passing years can't erase.

Fair hair (which she always said was too thin!)
Blue eyes, nice teeth, and an infectious grin.
Helped her with her homework as much as I could!
Both learning the piano (at which I was no good)

We were both fifteen when we first went out,
Our transport was by the local bus company.
A visit to a film show was an evening out,
Paid for by combining our pocket money.

An incident that I recall so well,
Was the occasion when we first held hands,
Running before the conductor rang his bell,
Hands locked in two joyous tingling bands.

'Boy, uxoriousness will be for you',
By my English master this was said.
I looked it up, and it came true,
For to Kathryn Shirley I am now wed.

Brian Reck

Spread Your Love

I do not have a fortune
I am not known for fame
But no-one could be happier
However great her name
Everyday of my life I thank God above
For a wonderful life of abundant love
I would not change with anyone
The life I have been given
For I'm sure I've been granted a little taste of heaven
So dear friends I wish you all
The joy and love I've known
Meet each day with a smile
Make your days worthwhile
And you will know a job well done.

Margaret Blackwell

On Valentine's Day

On romantic Valentine's beaus send red roses or cards with hearts
to the belles they love, just to say 'Only you are on my mind,
dreamt about day and night and I want you to be my Valentine.'

What's great about that day is that anyone can join in and celebrate
by giving to a chosen valentine a pleasant surprise of a special kind,
honour her as a fair queen, express all affection and care
to make her blossom with happiness and feel like walking on air.

Thus always on Valentine's a festive swing takes over the town
as if to signify that love makes the world go round.
And it's time to embrace and celebrate and celebrate!
Also that date sets my heart aglow and I find I want to live again.
'Cause another cheerful message it seems to entail,
that soon a brave, glorious Lady Spring is to come,
to unroll a floral carpet, lavishly decorated, for everyone.
It will delight the eye and the heart with blossoming fiery daffodils,
tulips, crocuses and many other gorgeous flowers.

You too, may be profusely showered for hours
with much sunshine, ready to kiss you, embrace
and caress with its warm rays,
powerful to generate all the enthusiasm you need to sprcad wings
and fly high to reach that star of your dreams.
So there's so much to celebrate on each Valentine's Day.

Lucy Carrington

DESTINY

My eyes sparkle bright and I can't hide
The warm feeling I have deep inside
It comes from the flame of desire
Once a small flicker, now risen higher

On my lips every kiss lingers
His soft touch tingles my fingers
I've felt our love grow each day
Now it takes my breath away

Something warm within my heart
Turns so cold when we're apart
But together we are one
Destiny is kind to some.

Clare Johnson

Love Search

My father left when I was small,
I cried so many tears,
I dreamed each night of his return
Through all my childhood years.

And so it was I fell in love -
At tender sweet sixteen,
With a dashing dark-eyed replica
Of photographs I'd seen.

It wasn't long before I knew
My body he'd adore,
But all the longing in my heart
He chose to just ignore.

So as the suitors came and went,
My inner longings grew,
Until one blinding moment -
On the day I first met you!

I felt I'd known you always,
And you had known me too,
We cared about each other's dreams
And shared each point of view.

Our friendship stood on solid ground
Before our love was born -
One magic, starry summer night -
You stayed with me till dawn.

And since that sunny morning,
With wide blue skies above,
We've laughed and cried together,
And *always* been in love.

Mary Tappenden

A Letter To Helena

I love you.
Je vous aime.
Such sweet words,
Such simple words,
In so many ways are taken,
In so many ways are spoken,
Yet, so many hearts are broken.

It has been said so often,
Beauty is in the eyes of the beholder.
How true my love, these words.
You are more lovely, more radiant
than a morning in June.
Your eyes are like to me, a treasure,
jewels in my crown.
You hair so like a feather
soft and rippling down.
Your skin to touch is velvet,
smooth and silk and warm.
Your hands caress so gently,
like waves upon the sands.
Your lips are tiny rosebuds,
that would touch upon my cheek.
So much kindness have you in your soul,
Oh, that we could meet.
But you ask, who am I?
That I cannot tell.
But only know, my dearest one,
I know thee, Oh, so well.

Jennifer Polledri

Thank You For Loving Me

Thank you for showing me love
A love which has transformed my life
Thank you for being there
In good times and in strife.

You revealed that goodness exists
A passion so strong, yet so pure.
A feeling of comfort and pleasure alike
The sense that you want me for sure.

Just when I thought the rain would never stop
The sun broke out and a rainbow brightened the sky.
In your eyes, I see all its colours.
It's certain, you're my guy.

I may not have told you in so many words,
However, believe me it's true.
Life has become so beautiful,
Now I'm sharing it with you.

Helen Georgeou

Love

I love you and I always will
Oh my beating heart be still
I run up the yard and wait by the gate
But I never get to see you because
You're always late

You are the sunshine in the rain
Please be my valentine again
Because you are so sweet
You make every day at school complete
And when the bell rings at half past three
Come over my house for chocolate cake
Made by me.

Rebecca Eira Davies

Though Spiders Ride The Wind

Though spiders ride the wind on silken skeins
And liquid breezes stir laburnum leaves,
Black sorrow in my heart remains
I cannot share these sunny days with you.

I dream of summers gone and passed away
When time was clothed in happiness and flowers
And misty mornings woke my eyes to you
I asked for nothing else from those sweet hours.

Our spirits matched - an ecstasy of love,
A link I thought eternity would stay
But now I dream yours rides the vaporous winds
And like the spider swings and drifts away.

Sandra Lewis

A Red Rose

I sent a red rose to my love
The one I call my gentle dove
The skin upon her cheek so fair
With golden ringlets for her hair
Her eyes are like forget-me-not blue
My love for her forever true
So here I stand my hand on heart
To swear that we will never part
Our hearts are light, young and gay
If only we can stay this way
But youth it starts to fade away
And middle years come to betray
My step is getting slower now
New seeds of love I have to sow
Although my heart it still beats true
A red rose I will send to you
Now that we are old and grey
Our love stays true as that first day
It started with a red, red rose
And to this day my love still shows.

Marjorie Spokes

A Dream Of Love

The rain like a curtain falls from the sky as she stepped
Through the open doorway, shaking her hair like a
Shaggy dog. I glance out of the open window at the rain
Caught, and held by the branches, divided into forked
Spears dripping. Then I turn my eyes,
Centre on her face again as she glides to the open
Fire letting her wet dress slide to the floor, like
A snake shedding its skin. Outside the loud wind is
Banging a window as she stands in the warm light shed
By the fire, stroking her soft white arms with her slender
Fingers. Letting her long brown hair fall softly,
Singing a quiet song to herself, sending a rushing
Fountain pounding through my veins. She always loved
The limelight so she sinks slowly to her knees as if
In a quiet prayer to herself, yet she means so much
To me, I dare not reach out to touch so I just
Looked on with tear filled eyes, because I am so
Afraid I may awaken and find her gone (vanished,
Like a phantom in a dream).

Cecil Cundell

FRIENDS NOT LOVERS . . .

I've always loved you,
Probably always will.
I pretend to run into you
As if I hadn't known that you'd be there
But had been hoping that you would.
When I see you I want you
But know I can't have you.
We've nearly made it but something holds us back.
Do you still care for her?
Are you scared of me hurting him?
I see how you look at me
I snatch a glimpse of you.
Every hug and kiss lasts longer than it should
Every look tells a story of more than friendship.
That's because there's been more, much more.
We can't go back, can't carry on
Can't think of anything but you.
And of how, if ever we could be together
It would work if it wasn't for the others
But I guess that's why we're friends not lovers . . .

Gill Price

PISCES

Born under the sign of the fish,
Slippery, sliding, sensual
Can you trust her?
You reach out to catch her in your hands
But she can drift out of sight,
Or twist herself around you
In an act of gasping tearing passion.
Pisces - sign of the unreliable
Airy, uncatchable,
Caring, dreaming, loving,
Her world is created within her.
See her smiling across a crowded room,
What is she really thinking?
Enjoy the moment my friend,
For a fish can dive out of sight
In a moment
To deep unfathomable oceans.

Judith Spencer

Love

Surrender mine endangered bliss
to thine enchanted cave.
Into a mould of you
I pour my liquid love
forever more.
Touch me, enlightened fool
Caress my loving
arms and warm embrace
Save my aching soul
Oh wondrous love.

Jaki Holden

UNTITLED

Last night was great and you were my
First date, you make me feel so brand new
When I'm with you. I hope you feel the same
Way too, when I first saw you standing
There, I knew then I cared, 'cos it happened.
That funny stare that made me look
And glare, I'd never felt this way, it
Makes me feel so happy and gay,
What did you do, what did you say to
Make me feel that way, you are my
One and only and I'll never be lonely
Love at first sight is what happened
That night, I finally saw the light
And it is pure delight.

D Devlin

LOVE

This is for you, my dearest love
I need to let my feelings show
I think of ways my love to prove
But in my heart I feel you know.

If you could see the tears I shed
Darling I miss you, miss you so
I think of all the joys we've shared
Since I first met you long ago.

Oh how I long to hear your voice
So pleased when that telephone rings
I'd rather see you, given choice
I'm sure you know the joy it brings.

My love for you goes on forever
Our love is such a precious thing
Could I stop? No never, never
I could not bear it ever ending.

Margaret Busst

Love's Garden

Love is a garden of delight
With blooms that last,
Even when out of sight,
Dug with caring thought,
Fed with effort
And watered with the tears of joy.
It is a journey of discovery
To wander through,
Each flower a moment
Of happiness or content
We have been privileged
To experience.

J M Butler

Like The Back Of Your Hand

I would like to be able to say
that I know something
like I know some things
like the back of my hand.

Do you know what that something is?
I think you know.

Will I ever know it?
Like some of those things
I want to know.

I want to know it,
will you let me know it?
Will I ever know it
as I know mine,

The back of your hand.

Colin Black

Loving You

When I touch your hand,
I am sent to a wonderland.
When you stand there,
Showing me you really care,
When my heart skips a miss,
Is when we kiss.
When we hold each other tight,
You make everything look bright.
When you stand by my side,
I have no hurt to hide.
Everything is so clear,
When you are near.
Our love is like the highest mountain,
And like a beautiful fountain.
Everything about you,
Makes my loving you grow.
'Cause to me you are the only one,
And every day is so much fun.
As your eyes say it all,
Which makes me stand tall!
'Cause loving you means a lot to me,
I don't care who can see.
What real loving means to us,
'Cause we don't make a fuss.
'Cause you are always there,
Showing love and how you care.
Showing tenderness,
Showing kindness.
In everything you do,
That is why I love you.

David Pickett

One Look At You

One look at you and I am lost for words to say,
One kiss from your sweet lips can take my breath away.
And I'm left wond'ring if you feel the same way too,
It happens every time I take one look at you.

One look at you and I see heaven in your eyes,
A moment in your arms can make me realise,
You're all I need to face each day anew,
It happens every time I take one look at you.

Across a crowded room I feel your eyes in search of mine,
And when they meet my heart stands still
It happens every time.

One look at you and I know you're the one for me,
No-one but you can make my dreams reality,
Enduring love like ours can last a lifetime through,
I see it every time I take one look at you.

Pauline Launt

ENDLESS LOVE

What now when one's beloved dies?
Our heart and soul filled with cries.
Cries of loss from the aching heart
For cruel fate caused love to part.

All that was shared now is naught,
Relief from such pain cannot be bought.
Each waking moment revives the hurt,
To know life's span ends so curt.

No words nor gestures can replace,
Each moment now without their face.
Material things have no meaning,
Naught can ease the pain now gleaning.

Here we are mortals but know this,
The spirit lives on and needs bliss.
Our beloved wants us not to mourn,
So let love in our heart once more born.

R Warrior

My Husband

I tremble with excitement
My knees begin to knock,
My heart beats so, I feel as though
I need to see the doc.

Adrenalin is pumping
My body feels all fizzy,
I feel so high, I'll hit the sky
I'm in an awful tizzy.

But hold on just a minute
The symptoms I'm revealing
Are all familiar, signs that say
I find you quite appealing.

Who has this power over me
Who makes me feel this way
When you're not there, I feel despair
You keep my fears at bay.

My soulmate, friend and lover
My other half and more,
Dear husband have I told you
It's you that I adore.

Carole Dicker

TIME WAS

I watch you from across the room
As though some stranger you might be.
The voice, the laugh, the caring touch
Are for another, not for me.

We met and loved in other times.
I knew those hands and lips so well;
Those shining days and honeyed nights
Melded together as in a spell.

When did our magic lose its way,
What truth best left unsaid was told?
When did laughter slip away
And hateful envy take its hold?

The hands of time will not reverse
Although I ache with deep regret,
Yet surely you can sense I'm near,
And feel the burn, as when we met.

You turn and see me, with a smile
Offering a hand that's strange and cool.
Your eyes appraise, assess and gaze.
But there's no yearning in their soul.

Somehow my lips refuse to say
What is expected - instead they shape
The saddest greeting from my heart -
'Too late, my love, too late'.

J Hawkes

GOODBYE

How does it feel to be going away?
The start of your 'dreams coming true'
I cannot imagine what, from this day,
Life's going to be like without you.

I know I said you'd never hurt me
but I didn't know you well then,
I never realised you'd turn out to be
the most wonderful of men.

Darling, I'm so happy for you
now that things are going your way.
Don't ever change, to your own self be true
All my love goes with you today.

Patricia Chilver

New Love

You are to me,
The unsavoured joy
Of a spring morning.
You are to me
The alluring mysteries,
Shadowed in a moon bewitched night.
Flesh demands.
Sharp as the bark
Of a predatory fox.
And as my bones melt,
With desire for you.
I wonder.
What am I to you my love?
Who am I to you?

Enid Phillips

CREATOR OF MY EDEN

I have lain dormant, untouched.
My soil's infertile,
left fallow and fruitless.
With only great stretches of unwoken emotion like barren desert,
to cloak my soul.

Your presence has sparked creation.
My body becomes alive with colours - sensation.
I swim in previously dammed oceans of exhilaration,
Then rise to take flight, filling my lungs with fresh anticipation.

My land is covered with the colours of life,
cerulean blue, pulsing aquamarine,
lush emerald interspersed with deep carmine.
Every newly born mountain and lake of devotion,
Beams at the creator of such intangible emotion.

As I orbit the maker of my garden of Eden,
I try to be wary of such immense freedom.
For the summit from which I view has a fall which is fatal
And I fear, my love, of what you are able.

Hannah Bird

LOVE

Four letters together spell out a word
Maybe you've used it, wrote it or heard
Somebody whisper its sound in your ear
Can stir you to passion,
Might incline you to fear,
Used by so many to woo and to wed
A favourite with lovers,
When snuggled in bed
A word used in songs, it's a lyricist's dream
It's a popular term used from Chester to Cheam
Languages call it a different name
To you and me though it's still the same flame
Burns in our hearts, kindling desire
Taking our dreams higher and higher
Love can be painful
Love can be bliss
Love can be simply a passionate kiss
Love is accepting your sister and brother
And making it up with your father and mother
It is the power that binds us together
Makes lovers swear
'I will love you forever'
Love has no limits,
Love has no fear,
Love is just saying
'I'm glad that *you're* here'.

Matthew Pearson

ALL I EVER WANT . . .

All I ever want to do
is just be close to you
All I ever want to say
is 'I love you' more each day
All I ever want to give
is my heart as long as I live
All I ever want to feel
is your love and affection and know it's real
All I ever want to know
is you'll always care and never let go.
All I ever want to be
is a 'special person' as you are to me
All I ever want to spend
is my time with you right to the end.

Maria Diana

Dream Desire

A passionate chase of a heart's embrace
the surreal touch of a physical desire

A lusted emotion thrusting inside
a volcanic thought that erupted untouched

A wild romance in a mindless trance
a desperate wanting you enter with caution

To bear your flesh contort for the taking
unaware if it's the right dissension you're making

Feeling the tingle from tip to toe
without being a corrupted soul

Fulfilling dreams where eyes have not seen
reflecting thoughts of desired beings

Visions in our mind are things we must hide
outside our thoughts we take no pride

Hold onto our dreams not wanting to wake
for dreams desire will certainly break

Wishing dreams to last forever
And life we endure to endeavour.

S Smith

THE LOVERS

Sunlight shines through the flowing fabrics, onto our bodies
Agleam with sweat and the sweet smell of love
From the kind of activity one does with one's lover.
The heat of the moment not long passed.

Hearts beating wildly, legs and arms entwined,
The touch of lips brushing skin.
Skin so soft, so smooth and yet so firm.

Sheets tossed aside, strewn across the floor,
Clothing abandoned in haste,
from the hall
to the bedroom
Tell us a tale of their own.

But now, upon the bed so divine.
Two souls no more, a unity has formed.
The surrendering to each other's passion
complete.
And now, this feeling of oneness
Being as close in the minds, as the bodies that touch.

Charlene Taylor

LOVE

Dirty socks in the laundry,
Three a.m feeds in the still of the night,
Flowers by a gravestone,
The first cuckoo of spring.

The morning rush to school,
A baby's first hesitant steps,
Fading photos - half-forgotten faces,
Long, warm summers evenings.

'What's for tea, mum?'
Happy splashings in the bath,
Stark TV images of war and famine,
The first frost of autumn.

A quiet moment, the house peaceful and still,
Small, tousled head on a pillow,
Memories of a sunset, far away,
A crisp winter morning of fresh falling snow.

All this, and more . . . my love.

Stella Duff

YOU

Time did stand still,
When I first saw you,
The background faded,
When I first saw you,
My heart began to race
When I first saw you
When we first met, face to face.

Other people ceased to be
When I first heard you,
Words turned to music,
When I first heard you.
Blood singing, in this case,
When I first heard you,
When we first spoke, face to face.

Your smile broke my heart,
When I first touched you
My skin burning,
When I first touched you,
Time changed its pace
When I first touched you
When we first touched, face to face.

My breath taken away,
When I first kissed you,
That tender first touch
When I first kissed you
Thought spinning in space
When I first kissed you
When we first kissed, face to face.

Many years later,
When I think of you,
My blood starts to sing
When I think of you
In a blissful state of grace
When I think of you
Will we ever meet again, face to face.

M Grigg

Valentine Message

Was it a dream or another lifetime?
Did you really love me?
We parted without a fond goodbye.
But still my heart remembers your warm loving eyes and tender smile.

We have not met for many many years
I've met others in other places, different faces, different smiles.
But only your face haunts me.
Only your smile warms me through all my life's trials.
You're my first love, you're my last love.
Only your love fills my lonely heart forever.
Though we may never meet again.
You're my only love and the best!
My dearest valentine.

Gwyneth Murphy

Leaving

I didn't wait for dawn
But rose in darkness
Leaving behind the slim
Figure still shrouded in
Sleep and half-light
And silently departing
Made my way through
Narrow streets not yet awoken
Thief-like not looking back
Or sideways
Hoping I would not meet
Or be met
Hoping enough was said
In the words unspoken
Hoping what wasn't
We could forget.

Richard Croke

I CAN'T DECIDE

Is this love? I cannot tell
It's a feeling new to me; warm and strange
I thought I knew what love was
a long time ago
But now that seems petty; just a teenage crush,
just a silly, childish thing
with no meaning.

This?
This is different;
a sensation I've never felt before.
Not tingling, lust, or going out to night-clubs,
taking drugs . . .
No. It's difficult to define.
A feeling of being out of control.
I'm almost afraid to let go
of him.

Scared too, of things unknown;
I can't allow myself to trust,
to let myself go,
to fall in love.
Perhaps those weeks and months in holidays,
with boys who hurt me,
twisted my mind, changed my life,
held my hand, touched me and said they loved me
have made me hard
to crack.

I want to love,
I wish so much I could.
I want to look into his shining eyes and say
I love you.
But I don't know if I do.

Kate Turner

Quiet Love

My love is a quiet love,
She whispers my name at the break of day,
Her gentle tone moves slowly toward my slumber,
To wake me full of love.

My love is a quiet love,
She gently kisses my lips,
To leave her soft breath upon my mouth,
To speak of all our love.

My love is a quiet love,
Her silent gaze looks into my soul,
Where she sees us both united,
Entwined in life and bound forever,
Our love is a quiet love.

Charles McGinness

My Partner

The taste of your lips is like nectar to me.
The smell of your body like wine.
I cannot perceive what my eyes see before me
Nor fully believe that you're mine.

Your hair black as coals, all shining and bright
And a smile showing teeth ivory white.
A form so fragile I hesitantly take
Into my arms so sure you'll break.

The years have flown by
Like me you have changed.
Outwardly put on a few pounds
Your hair, flecked with silver, is still shining bright
Your teeth, all yours, are still white.

I thank you for sharing your life day by day
Remaining the same as the day that we met
And look to the future following our way
With a love the same as we met.

Terry Baldwin

Love Makes No Sense

I feel you there I taste the thought
I sense your being, your smell haunts,
Drifting days, clouds in my mind
I wipe my eyes a thousand times.

I clench my face to stop the trembles,
my twisted thoughts are beyond reproach,
you wrenched my heart without redemption,
my happiness seduced by your soul.

I softly lay my head on your pillow
A silent aura fills my mind
Replacing my sadness,
Oh! how love is blind.

I love you now as I did then
My life is empty, I have no defence,
you left me demolished, a willow branch
mind and body in a dishevelled trance.

When will my misery end? . . .

S Jackson

MY VALENTINE

His eyes are blue and he's slim and tall,
We met New Year's Eve at the village hall.
The band played as we danced the night away,
He has such charm and poise, what will he say
If he sees me home will we meet again!
Are you going to be my valentine?

Wonder of wonders, he's written to me,
He's invited me out, where will it be?
I think I'll suggest dinner in town,
Am *I the one* or will he let me down?
I feel so happy and my heart's a flutter,
Are you going to be my valentine?

We met in the park, it was such bliss,
He held my hand, then gave me a kiss.
He said he loved me, did I feel the same?
I told him I'd willingly take his name,
So we now look forward to the great day;
He is going to be my valentine!

Eve de Groot

Dear Love

When you went away,
  And the trees wept in bitter spring green leaf,
My grief
  Was a lonesome thing.
For a brief, brief moment, only me,
And you no longer there,
To share enchanting new found depths
  Of dear delight.

When you returned
  The trees were bare,
And I was aware
  Of you then,
And that other older time
When the blood ran young, and sang,
With deep, deep, long lost dreams
  Of you and me.

Now you are here
  The trees full blown,
Unknown
  The anguish of that final parting.
I can believe in you now,
And youth, sweet, sad, sad youth, long gone,
Looks on, and dreams again
  Of you, dear love.

Pamela Gooding

The One I Love

To thee I love I owe my all,
From your side my heart will call,
From your arms my body cold,
From your lips a kiss to hold.

My empty heart you always fill,
Within your arms you warm it still,
Together touch and dream of this,
You take my breath with treasured kiss.

So hold me tight, so near, so close,
As if our hearts are one,
Where temptation fears to walk,
Your arms where I belong.

Victoria Elliott

Misty Morning Valerie

Wild flower of the hedgerow
Most beautiful of flowers,
You look so pale and fragile
In the morning's misty hours -
Your image stays fresh in my mind
Just like a girl I know,
My misty morning Valerie
Wild flower of the hedgerow.

K Newport

My Love

I love you like the summer sun
that warms you through and through,
I love you like the autumn
that soothes and pampers you,
I love you like the winter
that wraps you round like snow,
And I love you like the springtime
that renews old urges so.
And I will always love you
wherever I may be,
You'll always be my sweetheart
and mean everything to me,
And when this life is over
I'll know I'm truly blessed,
If you're by my side in heaven
and in my place of rest . . .

A Clark

The Chains Of Love

If I could hold you in my arms
I would never let you go
I could love you all my life
But you will never know

You left me for someone else
That you had loved before
You thought your feelings for her had gone
But they came back to haunt once more

She had ended it with you
As she too loved another
So you know there is no chance
Of getting back together

So now each night I lay alone
And I know you do as well
Both of us wanting the one we can't have
Both living a life of hell

I love you and you love her
Neither having their way
We both hope against the odds
Our loved one comes back to stay

I pray your love for her will die
And you'll return to me once more
To love me more that you did her
What else is my life for?

Until then my heart is chained
I cannot love another
I must stay in purgatory
Hoping we get back together.

Bernice Evans

Four Words

In the loneliness and darkness
Four words can light up your life

The way the beach is kissed by the sea
Flowers highlighted by the morning sun
The grass is kissed by the morning dew
Two birds sing at the onset of dawn's light

To hold you is pure pleasure
Your smile is joy and happiness
With eyes so soft and gentle
And touch so light and loving

To cradle you is to love you
Hold close - unbelievable pleasure
To caress your skin - and look within
At a heart full of love and joy

When the whole world just seems full of pain
These words will lift up life again
Will give your life a sense of meaning
And a feeling of love - and well being

These four words are no secret
Thirteen letters all in all
But because they are said with meaning
No other things can see to harm you

These four words will always be within
For these four words will stay for life
These four words are the best - they are
I love you daddy.

Keith Morgan

My Love

If it should be that I should lose your love,
The sun would vanish from the sky above.
If you should leave your place, here at my side,
My broken heart from all I could not hide.
If never more your sweet voice I should hear,
No other sound would ever ring so clear.
If I no more your lovely face could see,
No-one again will win a smile from me!
The air would cool - no warmth could flourish here,
Unless you bring it with your presence dear.
Life would be dull - no purpose would I see
Without your love to help and comfort me.
I do not think that I could love you more,
And I have never loved like this before.
You fill my world, like stars and moon and sun,
I sing your praise to each and everyone.
For you no task I would refuse to do,
If it would bring delight and joy to you!
So end my torment - give my heart some hope,
That with my busy life I still can cope.
Return my love, and in my future reign,
And I will never, never want for aught again!

Barbara Hussey

AN OPENING

I gave you my key
a symbolic gesture maybe -
to open an inner door
to see if you liked what's inside.

A key to my home
where I feel comfortable and free -
to be me,
just in case I needed you
and you wanted me.

Does this key open my heart you ask?
You'll find it in the looking
the knowing
the seeing -.

No words will tell you
Only the eyes have the answer.

Christine Rogers

STARLINGS

These people speak in tongues,
Strange dialects I do not understand.
Those words I catch are thin and raw,
Dull dialling tones of work and rain
And children's ailments.
But on this morning
When the fields are silver with the spider's work
A starling sits upon the line
Which feeds the country with this village brogue
And chats a sonnet to his mate,
So every word which leaves this place
Becomes
A
Love
Song.

Ben Verinder

Love Is . . .

Love is but an ocean
Waving far and near.
Wanting someone always
To love and take all fear.

Love is but a mountain
A mountain we all climb.
Longing to hold that someone
To call that someone mine.

Love is but a challenge
To see life through with love.
To cherish someone down below
To love those up above.

Rebekah Hudson

Our Love Is True

I looked upon you like peace
If like a bird in the sky
Quiet and loving
Next to stars
Elegant in many ways
So much love
You bring into my days
Words can't describe

A queen in your own world
Dressed in your own hand-made gown
Even when I'm down
You bring light
In my dreams I can't explain
Deep inside my heart
I carve out your name

Our love is special
The fire in the flame
Still burns for you
Our love is true
Together as one
Never to part
My darling Maryanne
You burn a torch in my heart.

Ricky McNeill

Dark Horse

I've been following up your looks and style,
As I've been engrossed by your subtle smile.
I'm going back to when you asked me for a dance,
In your arms was to feel entranced.
I was holding a body so gorgeous and divine,
That in my wishful thinking hoped you were mine.
Beauty be held in your youthful face,
Shimmering with that of a heavenly trace.

When in your company I was last,
My presence was taken away all too fast.
I was diverted by an uncaring lust,
In one I should not have placed my trust,
She took my love and threw it in the air,
But I could catch and took it elsewhere.
To lose an untrustworthy lust,
I hope to gain favour in your trust.
I've been eager for your love for so long,
But if ever I make a move it goes so wrong.
To you is where I wish to centre my attention,
And offering you my general affection.

Dragon

Untitled

Oh valentine
Where art thou
You should have phoned
But don’t try now
You’ve missed out
As soon you’ll see
For I’m too good
For the likes of thee

Elaine Briscoe-Taylor

Regrets

I sleep, eat and drink your name,
Although we may never love again.
I had your love but let it go,
For reasons you may never know.

I loved you then, I love you now,
We were set to take the sacred vow.
Like most great loves we had the storms,
But even so we had no qualms.

Out times of bliss quite outweighs,
The number of our unhappy days,
I hope sometimes when you are alone,
You think of happy days at home.

If you can't forgive me don't forget,
For hurting you so I'll forever regret.
When you love you do with all your heart,
What a fool I was to let us part.

My only wish I hope and pray,
We will be together again some day.
If this should be, I'll be supreme,
With you beside me like a queen.

But it's better to love and lose some day,
Than never to be in love they say.

J Hopkins

Forever There

You are a river that flows through my heart,
you've been with me from the start.
So deep and so dark,
you have surely left your mark.
Oozing softly through my life,
always there beside me, my loyal and trusting wife.
From the tiny childhood streams,
unfulfilled dreams,
to the adult ocean waves,
that will stir me until the grave.
Your bitter, shivering poison, like a drug it addicts me,
ever on your door I'll knock, my soul predicts me.
You are so rare,
and will always be forever there.

Glenn B Liddle

Precious Time

I pledged to you my heart and soul
To love you forever would be my goal
We made together this sacred vow
This love to die we'd never allow

Yet people keep their love so pure
But human life cannot endure
Immune we're not to years of age
Time together you cannot gauge

The life-line there upon your palm
Nature's scar of inflicted harm
The young today still don't know
How quick their life is soon to go

So I tell you now enjoy each day
And let the old be on their way
And maybe even spare a smile
Making life itself a lesser trial

Josephine Aldred

FELICITY

In the moment came a vision clean
Of windswept pines and England's green
Cliffs o'erlooking a laughing sea
Tumbling, white-crested, jollily
Caressing amber sand.

Then I heard my own heartbeat
Above the throb of the city's street
All noise dimmed down to murmuring rain
I was conscious only of lingering pain
In a far-flung alien land.

I write her name . . .
A tolling bell of tired morbidity
Becomes a silver cataract of flame

Bryn Bartlett

Card To Angel's Camp - USA

(To Jim Hayes)

You held the card, Tuesday you
said, of Rosetti'e triptych tale
that I'd sent across the world
to you there in Angel's Camp,
feeling you, me, all one united,
in the ecstasy of that sudden kiss
depicted by Pre-Raphaelite hand.
'Time' was undone; it seemed
our tale as much as those lovers
there.
The scene showed a lady dressed in dark blue,
seated pious (I thought reading holy works)
reaching upwards, eager, book suddenly askew,
under coloured glass window, meeting her knight's
downward, inflaming kiss.
And this 'time round' re-capturing all
that never was 'lost in paradise'
will we be merciful to their martyrdom,
. your wife, your friend in
love's old story, of forbidden lady fair.
We said we were without worldly faults
truth seeking, Godly, pure; yet what
truths can we boast of now?
Will I draw back from you, and 'sleep'
once more, or inevitably draw close to a kiss
of Camelot proportion,
observed by Dante, Virgil,
as the two pictured lovers will we float willingly to Hell,
after our determined embrace,

Allyson Kennedy-Kiddle

You

I sit here in a daze,
Dreaming of only you.
You seem so perfect,
Your innocence, your smile,
Only you could be
The one for me.

I loved you so,
Your kisses and wine,
Tasted so fine!
Now, I remember why!
You were not perfect,
You seduced me fine!

After all the wine,
The men and the women,
Who do you consider
The most seductive
Of them all?
Was it me, perhaps?

Tammara M Wilband

I TRULY DO

We all do ask what is love,
A mystery, a miracle or only nature,
Love driven by biology
Or by aesthetic preference,
Perhaps by hedonistic lust
Or simply human need of company,
But none of these can explain
Why I love you, my darling,
Or you love me so faithfully
Amid all the many that we meet
In our hurly burly lives,
So what is love that defies reason,
I will never know the cause,
But I love you, dearest heart,
I know I truly do.

Richard Reeve

THERE WAS A SOUL

there was a soul
that once I touched
moments of time stood still
the warmth the glow the inner peace
the feeling felt by none around
being one was truly divine
this whole being was not denied

now worlds apart
there is a longing
but through kin there is no way in
hours of thought in this decision
travels abroad and physical submission

occasionally a call will come
pleasantries and polite conversation
but the truth is still carried within
occasionally the truth breaks out
but only through the windows to within

Gabley Copperston

I Miss You

I miss you and I want you all of the while,
From your cheeky grin,
Through tears of joy,
Most of all your deep set smile.

Without switching lights on you illuminate any room that you're in,
This light it radiates quite brightly,
Never in the shadows at lowest you could call it dim,
Above all darkness,
Never nightly.

This light feels its way into people's hearts, every single day,
Growing constantly with time it never departs,
Linking the two of us in no other way.

This love that we share bonds time after time whenever we set up the pace,
Please get home safely and don't forget, you have already won,
It was never a two horse race.

Stephen Maughan

I Look At You As Through A Window . . .

I look at you as through a window
At a summer's day
A day so fair, a sky so blue
But clouds not far away.

My spirit lifts, I would rejoice
And yet I know so well
That if I venture to the sun
The storm I'll live to tell.

You are indeed a summer's day
And none could be as fair
The bluest skies are in your eyes
And sunshine is your hair.

I look at you as through a window
Longing to be near
With the warmth I am at one
It is the storm I fear.

For capricious is a summer's day,
But speak and it will rain
The lightning strikes, the oak tree falls
And joy is turned to pain.

I wish with all my heart I could
But keep the clouds at bay
And if but for a little while
Love that summer's day.

Jack Crossman

Love Of My Life

Slumped, sleeping in a soft armchair.
Once handsome, vibrant, with thick dark hair,
now white, thinning, caressing worry lines.
Bi-focals, limp limbs, other ageing signs.

Football, now a sleeping potion from the telly.
Cup of tea balanced on a growing pot belly.
Newspaper abandoned, crossword incomplete;
interest lost, energy low, retires to favourite seat.

Soon refreshed he'll waken, with sparkling eyes anew.
Fifty-six years of weathering, gone like summer dew.
Springs to his feet, reaches out to me, his wife;
suggests an interlude upstairs. Love of my life.

Gibson Forbes

Love's Old Story

Love is the sweetest thing,
So the lilting song goes,
But everyone knows,
It isn't all complete happiness.
When partners begin to criticise,
And tempers start to rise,
Making up might compensate
If you do not leave it too late,
To kiss and cuddle
Laughing at the muddle,
You and your mate
Helped to create,
So drop your pride
And decide to say 'sorry,'
Before the sun is set
You won't regret,
To start a new day,
In the old, affectionate way,
And you will find
Peace of mind.
For what else can bring such bliss,
When you kiss and say,
'Darling, in my own selfish way,
I love you, I truly do,
Believe me, what else
Can there be,
Than love's old story
For you and me.'

Philip J Ellis

Where Did Love Go?

Did our love just drift away
Did we really let it go
Without even a parting tear
To mark the hour, the day, the year.

Can it be our love was just a fragile flower
And faithfulness, and deep fond friendship
Is not the power that can sustain
And nourish the tenderness that love alone obtains.

Or is true love an ever-changing theme
That we mere mortals seek in vain
The thrilling touch, the gentle word of yesteryear
Never to understand the value of a newer love
That can be just as real with but a different pain.

A love that lies beneath the surface
Awaiting time to blossom once again
Freed from frenzied early passion
But just as true yet in another frame.

The time must come my darling
When, clinging tightly to each other
We will know the new true love
That binds together 'til time has gone
And hearts beat once again as one.

Edgar Wall

LOVE . . .

Love is an emotion that we all have felt,
And depends really on the cards that are dealt,
But in order to love, you can't always have your way,
But then love, if it's real, can be for forever and a day.
Love is the strongest of all your feelings,
If can pick you up, and help you with your dealings,
But hate is the easier path to follow,
So feel it if you must, in times gone by,
That in order to love, you must learn how to cry,
Crying shows that you truly feel,
And shows to everyone, that your love is real.
So if you love, and your feelings are true,
Everything you give will be given back to you,
Love is truly a precious thing,
Not quite unlike a wedding ring.
Sometimes when you love, people will laugh,
Then tread on you with their terrible wrath,
They think that their way makes them quite cool,
But can't they see, that they are the fool.
So if you believe, and your love is true,
You'll never find yourself feeling blue,
So please believe that love is the way,
And your life'll be full of light, like the sun in May.
So if you've taken in everything I've said,
And you've understood everything you've read,
Your look of life will be truly full of light,
And your understanding of things will reach a new height.

Glen Johnson

Au Revoir

I held contentment in my hands
But let it slip my grasp,
Yet knew when we first started
My fortune couldn't last.

I'll amble on as best I can
And some day I'll forget,
The pain I felt as you slipped away
And the joy when we first met.

My only hope is maybe
You'll remember me somehow,
With warmth and fond affection
Though you're not with me now.

Take care and please be happy
As you travel near and far,
'Cos for me this is not farewell
But merely 'Au Revoir . . .'

Ashley P Loasby

A DESCRIPTION OF MY TRUE LOVE

Not the manliest of men that may be true,
But all that could make me happy he'd do.
A Godlike body - he has not,
But a body that satisfies me he's got.
No Arnold Schwarzenegger shaped arms,
He doesn't need muscles - for he bulges with charms.
Intellects may call him a dope,
But throw him any problem and he'll cope.
He may never come up with the common cold cure,
But of his love for me - he makes me sure.
Trivial Pursuit he'd rather not play,
But on racing or football he's got plenty to say.
Love poems or sonnets I seldom get,
But birthdays and anniversaries he's never forgot.
When things go wrong he may get frantic,
But that's the other side of a true romantic.
To say our love's perfect wouldn't be true,
But we love each other enough to see anything through

Shirley Ann Downing

Duty Kisses

You kiss me *goodbye* and kiss me *hello*
But your kiss has no meaning and so,
Although my lips cling in an effort to bring
Some life and some loving back into your eye,
It's *goodbye.*

This note is to say that as you leave me today
With a meaningless kiss I am telling you this
I have decided to give your *hello* a miss
For a kiss should mean something even although
It is only, sincerely, *goodbye.*

I M Williams

THE OLD SAILOR

I asked an old sailor, about his life,
where was he born?
Did he ever have a wife?
'I was born in Hull, a seaport so fair,
my wife was so pretty, with long golden hair.
But we drifted apart like ships in the night.
So I put out to sea, with seagulls in flight,
I'm a man on my own, a man of the sea.
From a village up north, the port of Whitby.
It's really not fair, as the sea's in my blood,
women as friends are okay by me,
but you can't separate a man from the sea.'

A T Lammiman

I Remember You

I remember the feeling
Of holding you near,
I remember the feeling
As you shed a tear,
I remember the feeling
Of your breath on my face,
I remember the feeling
Of your touch and your taste,
I remember the way
You held me in your gaze,
And now I yearn for
Our last loving days.

Darren Moody

WRONG

Why is it wrong
To love you

Why is it wrong
To want to be yours

Why is it wrong
To want you to hold me

Why is it wrong
To want to
Gently kiss your hand
And gaze into your eyes

O why is it wrong to love you

Marda

LOVE

Absent from me, I go insane,
I need you here to relieve the pain,
Driving inside of me, I need your touch,
To satisfy my emptiness, in my clutch.
I promise I will do no wrong,
If you continue to hold me strong.
I love you more than life itself,
Giving my heart a whole new health.
Your kind words and gentle caress,
Mean I feel more, by no means less.
The words I say and those which I write,
Should hopefully shed some light.
On feelings I hold, the amount I care,
So please let's remain, our hearts never to tear.

Melissa Perez

What Is Love

What is love?
Is it what I feel
When I think of you?
The affection deep inside of me,
The emotions making me happy,
The warmth, tenderness and passion
You give to me.
The devotion I want to give you,
The precious feeling inside of me
the frustration I show, when I can't see you.
The smile I get when I daydream
The shy sensation I gain
When I talk to you.
The closeness between us,
The romance I dream of
The temptation of being with you
The amazing daze I'm in.
The fascination and yearning
The fantasy world I'm living in
Is this love I'm feeling?

Danielle Turner

LOVERS

Nobody can alter, lovers are we,
Sharing our lives together, you, me.
Making a home a little love nest,
Where we can sit and relax and rest.
Holidays abroad, in the hot sun,
We have good times loving, lots of fun.
Listening to music until we tire,
Cold winters snuggled up by the fire.
Can't believe we would want another,
All we wish, is to be with each other.
Our love together really is strong,
Please, please, don't let it go wrong.
Worship one another until our dying breath,
Sharing this feeling until our death.

Ann Dulon

381

Tenderly holding you, until your fears subside
Holding your hand, stroking you, being by your side
Running my fingers gently over your beautiful frame
Every delicate touch, setting my soul and body aflame
Every touch another brush stroke on my canvas of love

Events have completely overtaken me, I am left enthralled
Into my life you have broken and my emotions that were walled
Gain fresh hope and enthusiasm for a source of joy so rare
Hardly daring to speak your name, laying all my love out bare
Touch me tenderly, my dreams are fragile but within reach

Only let me have time to show you how good it could be
Never to need anyone else, knowing you'd always have me
Enter into an Eden with me and stay forever.

Roseanna May

Lack Of Love

We are in a world of love it seems
Even though there is shattered dreams,
People always want to share,
Trying so very hard to care,
Sometimes easy, sometimes hard,
Sometimes feel your life's left scarred.
Give a little, take some more,
Look at people we all adore,
Hold them tight, within your heart,
And try to make a fresh new start.

L Marshall

He Does Not Know

There's something in his smile, something in his walk,
something in his stance, something in the way he talks.
There will never be another, who could make me feel this way,
I think of him constantly, my thoughts, they fill my day.
I wish I could approach him, tell him how I feel,
tell him that it's not a crush, my feelings they are real.
But he's a rising star and I am just a fan,
I sit alone for hours, working on my plan.
Next time that I see him, I'll tell him face to face,
that in my heart, for always, he will have a place.
But he passes me by, with that smile, the one that makes me weak,
I sit and stare and stutter, now quite unable to speak.
So I keep these feelings to myself, my feelings which are true,
I wonder if I'll go to my grave, wishing he had knew.

L Higgins

QUESTIONS

I live in a dream
Alone with the past
I keep asking the question
Why doesn't love last?

I can't forget you
Although I really do try
I keep asking the question
What made our love die?

I know that it's over
But I still feel the pain
I keep asking the question
Will I see you again?

I know you're unhappy
As I wait by the phone
I keep asking the question
When will you come home?

The questions come easily
But the answers aren't clear
For love is the truth
The reason we're here

But if love fades
With a passion turned cold
We can only reflect on the past
As we slowly grow old

William L I Newman

Love Has Flown

I'm feeling particularly grumpy,
I haven't had a girlfriend for years.
Perhaps because I'm small and dumpy,
Perhaps because I'm big on ears.
I've been married twice, believe it or not,
But my first wife dumped me, and then,
I went and tied a second knot,
Then I got dumped again.
I suppose that I'm something of a wet,
Far too boring, far too mellow.
Yet, I wish I could sing like *Wet, Wet, Wet*,
And look like that Pellow fellow.
Yes, I was a minor pop star once,
but love put me out to grass,
Now I'm unable to smile at girls,
whilst my teeth sing to themselves in their glass.

Bruce Ward

Journey

What road is this
my heart takes
once again?
Can it be love or
just a fitful fever?
my mind besotted
by your being -
fearful of your absence.
This place,
a painful memory
because you were here
with me - once,
and now are gone
like the morning mist.

Peter Cranswick

Words Unspoken

Somewhere in the storm of my life
It stopped raining,
Was warm,
It was you.

Sometime, in my not so young years
The clock stopped,
Time stood still,
It was you.

Somehow, when I thought my life broken
It became whole,
Restored,
It was you.

Someday I will find the right words to say to you
For giving me life, love
And freedom,
Thank you . . . it was you.

Mary Brooke

MORE FISH IN THE SEA

Of six billion people living on earth,
everyone of them was unique at birth,
so strangely odd and wonderfully true,
that I fell in love with a fish like you.

For I was daft and longed for romance,
someone to talk with and maybe to dance,
but you were so cold and ill at ease,
declining to court or even to please.

From what I've said it'll be no surprise,
that my choice of love was silly not wise,
but I've heard it said that love is blind,
and now I can't get you out of my mind.

I dreamt of love only till you I'd seen,
at a dancing school in smart Kensal Green,
but you just ignored me waiting there,
and smiled at a mermaid with beautiful hair.

Alas now my hair is shorn clean away,
and from Kensal Green I have travelled today,
across the wide world to swim in a dream,
with neither a home nor a job nor a scheme.

I could change my mind from fat become thin,
hoping forever your love I might win,
but I think I'll forget you in time and instead,
fish for a merman who'll take me to bed.

Delia Marheineke

From The Darkness

Before his presence kissed my cheek, I was all alone,
Empty were my thoughts, my heart as hard as stone.
To love was to trust, but to trust was to cry,
For, shattered were my hopes, existing only to die.
My life was filled with sorrow, my tears as cold as ice,
Feelings torn to shreds, heartache like bitter spice.
Colour drained of vitality, sun robbed of warmth,
Blood boiling with anger, an envy pushing forth.
Whimpering through the rough, a flower fading without trace,
But, good beginning to weave satin silk with patterned lace.
Beauty so spectacular, aspirations to draw me in,
Something new to revive dead emotion, to search the soul within.

He's like a breath of fresh air in a world of delusion,
Honesty without deception, love pure without confusion.
Wispy strands of cotton velvet falling around his face,
Eternal warmth and security from arms of gentle grace.
Balls of piercing sapphire charm glowing like steaming ember,
Marzipan fingertips to hold and caress, fidelity lasting forever.
Curling creepers of brittle yarn, upwards delving out,
Lips to graze innocent lives, though spirit wavering in doubt.
Shirt collar stained with scented dreams, skin tainted with manly
bristle,
Entwining words of ribboned respect, no plunging in of sharpened
thistle.
A lesson to gain in sugary young lust, just a passion without
design,
But, Utopia dies within me; this man can never be mine.

Karen Mather

UNTIL

Until my heart stops beating within my heaving breast;
Until the wind takes, from my lips, my final dying breath.
Until the summer turns to winter and the seas run dry;
Until the final tear has fallen from my weeping eye.
Until the sun stops burning and the sky has lost its blue;
Until that day has dawned, my love, I will always love you.

Until the stars stop shining and the winds no longer blow;
Until the deserts freeze and the rivers no longer flow.
Until the moon has fallen and endless night begun;
Until the polar ice-cap melts beneath a blistering sun.
Until the mountains crumble and fall into the sea,
Until the day has dawned, my love, I will always love thee.

Martin Goldsmith Silk

The Grand Romancer

The Grand Romancer casts his highest spell,
But once, and only once upon each heart,
And grants the deepest wishes of the soul
When all love's truths he magically imparts.

He seeks two hearts, two souls that are alike,
That share a deep affinity when matched,
Then weaves his way in secret, through their dreams
And draws them close with powers unsurpassed.

He moves from dream to dream with subtle care,
Whispering incantations as he goes,
And fills the air that separates the two,
With hints exquisite, so far unbeknown.

And chanting sweet enchantments all the while,
He softly whispers out his gloried spell,
Whilst placing in between the two, the window of all wisdom,
Through which they view each other as reflection of themselves.

Betwixt the two, he builds a magic land,
In which he lives when night must yield today.
From here he interlaces strands of life with strands of love
And twines them round two hearts, two souls to bind them in all ways.

No matter how they twist and turn and writhe,
In frantic effort, trying to make escape,
The Grand Romancer holds them with his charms,
Until two hearts, two souls, accept their destiny, their fate.

As the high and noble keeper of true love,
He holds all knowledge - truth within him lays,
So till his wondrous spell has took effect,
E'er in his magic land, and dreams, the Grand Romancer stays.

Emily Johnson-Rodgers

The Span

When love is gone
With the wave, washed out
Breaking the song
The seagulls squeak their knife edge song,
cutting the rhythm . . .
But hush, a beam, the morning sun.

Hope, warmth, mellow, before
the fire burns.

Pat Jones

INFORMATION

We hope you have enjoyed reading this book - and that you will continue to enjoy it in the coming years.

If you like reading and writing poetry drop us a line, or give us a call, and we'll send you a free information pack.

Write to :-

Anchor Books Information
1-2 Wainman Road
Woodston
Peterborough
PE2 7BU
(01733) 230761